How to Reduce your Carbon Footprint

Amanda Bishop

Crabtree Publishing Company

www.crabtreebooks.com

Crabtree Publishing Company

www.crabtreebooks.com

Author: Amanda Bishop
Coordinating editor: Chester Fisher
Series and project editor: Shoreline Publishing Group LLC
Project Manager: Kavita Lad (Q2AMEDIA)
Art direction: Rahul Dhiman (Q2AMEDIA)
Design: Ranjan Singh (Q2AMEDIA)
Photo research: Akansha Srivastava (Q2AMEDIA)
Editor: Ellen Roger
Copy editor: Mike Hodge
Project editor: Robert Walker
Production coordinator: Katherine Kantor
Prepress technician: Katherine Kantor

P3: Corbis (bottom left), Istockphoto (bottom right); P4: Tony Tremblay / Istockphoto; P5: Broker / Dreamstime (top); P5: Warren Faidley / Photolibrary (bottom); P6: Ed Pritchard / Getty Images; P7: Hans Georg Eiben / Photolibrary; P8: Alan Thornton / Getty Images; P9: ALBERTO CESARGREENPEACE / Associated Press; P10: Jocelyn Augustino / FEMA; P11: US Coast Guard; P12: Q2aMediaImage Bank; P13: David R. Frazier / Photolibrary (top); P13: STILLFX / Shutterstock; P14: ROMEO GACAD / Staff / AFP / Getty Images; P15: Jim West / Alamy; P16: VOLKER STEGER / SCIENCE PHOTOLIBRARY; P17: Mermet / Photolibrary; P18: Juriah Mosin / Shutterstock; P19: Fred Dimmick / Istockphoto (middle); P19: Tony Tremblay / Istockphoto (bottom);

P20: Energy Star (top); P20: Tomas Loutocky / Shutterstock (bottom); P21: Q2amedia Image bank (top); P21: Wayne Eardley / Getty Images (bottom); P22: Airbus S.A.S 2007; P23: ATW Photography / Photolibrary (top); P23: McCoy Aaron / Photolibrary (bottom); P24: Manoj Valappil / Shutterstock; P25: WizzyWig Images / Alamy; P26: Bervivo / Shutterstock (top); P26: Arthur Tilley / Getty Images (bottom); P27: Marc Vérin / Photolibrary; P28: MARTIN BOND / SPL / Photolibrary; P29: J-Charles Gérard / Photononstop / Photolibrary (bottom); P29: Dita Alangkara / Associated Press (top); P30: Michael Ventura / Alamy (Top); P30: Dita Alangkara / Associated Press (bottom); P31: ELISE AMENDOLA / Associated Press.

Cover: Don and Liysa King/Stone/Getty Images
A family plants a small tree. Tree planting helps to replace trees used by man for industry.

Title page: Istockphoto
Blue sky over solar panels at a small solar power station.

Library and Archives Canada Cataloguing in Publication

Bishop, Amanda
    How to reduce your carbon footprint / Amanda Bishop.

(Energy revolution)
Includes index.
ISBN 978-0-7787-2918-1 (bound).
--ISBN 978-0-7787-2932-7 (pbk.)

    1. Environmental protection--Citizen participation--Juvenile literature. 2. Sustainable living--Juvenile literature. 3. Global warming--Prevention--Juvenile literature. I. Title. II. Series.

TD171.7.B58 2008   j640   C2008-901524-X

Library of Congress Cataloging-in-Publication Data

Bishop, Amanda.
    How to reduce your carbon footprint / Amanda Bishop.
      p. cm. -- (Energy revolution)
    Includes index.
    ISBN-13: 978-0-7787-2932-7 (pbk. : alk. paper)
    ISBN-10: 0-7787-2932-X (pbk. : alk. paper)
    ISBN-13: 978-0-7787-2918-1 (reinforced library binding : alk. paper)
    ISBN-10: 0-7787-2918-4 (reinforced library binding : alk. paper)
    1. Energy conservation--Juvenile literature. 2. Greenhouse gas mitigation--Juvenile literature. 3. Environmental protection--Juvenile literature. 4. Atmospheric carbon dioxide--Juvenile literature. I. Title. II. Series.

TJ163.35.B58 2008
621.042--dc22

         2008012082

Crabtree Publishing Company

www.crabtreebooks.com   1-800-387-7650

Published in Canada
Crabtree Publishing
616 Welland Ave.
St. Catharines, ON
L2M 5V6

Published in the United States
Crabtree Publishing
PMB16A
350 Fifth Ave., Suite 3308
New York, NY 10118

Published in the United Kingdom
Crabtree Publishing
White Cross Mills
High Town, Lancaster
LA1 4XS

Published in Australia
Crabtree Publishing
386 Mt. Alexander Rd.
Ascot Vale (Melbourne)
VIC 3032

Contents

Energy Conservation: "We Can Do It!"

"We Can Do It" was a slogan that appeared on posters made during World War II. One poster featured "Rosie the Riveter," a woman dressed in blue coveralls (shown below). The poster was originally intended to encourage women to enter the workforce in industry to replace the men who left to serve in the war. Today, the image of Rosie the Riveter represents a time when people came together as a society to reach a common goal. Today's energy challenge can be combatted in a similar way. Together, we can work to save our planet from the pollution caused by burning **fossil fuels** by learning to conserve energy and developing alternative energy sources.

Energy Works

Heat, light, sound, and motion are some common forms of energy. Scientists define energy as the capacity to do work. People use energy every day to power machines such as vehicles, stoves, refrigerators, and air conditioners.

Energy Changes

Energy cannot be created or destroyed, but it can be converted, or changed from one form to another. People have learned to change energy from one form to another to make it do work for them. For example, light energy is converted into electrical energy to run your solar-powered calculator. In power plants, energy changes its form to generate power. The power is then directed to homes, schools, and businesses in the form of electrical energy, or electricity.

Straight to the Source

Energy comes from many sources. The Sun is a source of heat and light energy. Wind and water are sources of **kinetic energy**, or energy from motion. These energy sources are **renewable** energy sources. Their supply of energy is unlimited. Other energy sources are **non-renewable**. Their supply is limited. Once the supply is used up, there is nothing to replace it. Fossil fuels are a non-renewable energy source. Fossil fuels include oil, gas, and coal.

Power lines transmit electricity to homes, schools, and businesses. Electricity allows people to cook food, run machines, and heat and cool buildings.

Fossil Fuels

Today, humans get much of the energy they use by burning fossil fuels. In many parts of the world, fossil fuels are used to power automobiles. We run lights and appliances on electricity generated by burning coal. We heat our homes by burning **natural gas**. All of this non-renewable energy use adds up. Human energy use, especially the burning of fossil fuels for energy, has serious effects on our environment.

(right) Wind turbines use wind, a renewable source of energy, to produce electricity. The use of wind turbines is growing worldwide.

(below) Fossil fuels are used so frequently that many people never stop to think about where they come from or how much we actually use them.

Energy Challenges

Cars burn fossil fuels and cause air pollution in the form of smog.

There are challenges involved with all types of energy, both renewable and non-renewable. Renewable energy, such as solar and wind power, are not available when the sun is not shining or the wind is not blowing. Non-renewable sources, such as coal, oil, and natural gas, are difficult to find and collect. They also create pollution when they are burned. Nuclear energy is generated with uranium, a non-renewable resource. It does not cause air pollution, but it does produce **radioactive waste** that must be disposed of safely.

Depending on Fossil Fuels

People all over the world depend on fossil fuels for energy. Most power plants burn fossil fuels, and most cars and trucks run on gasoline or diesel fuel. Most homes are heated by burning oil, gas, or coal. Burning fossil fuels creates air pollution and emits carbon dioxide (CO_2).

Using Fossil Fuels

Fossil fuels must be **extracted**, or removed from the ground, and **refined**, or processed into usable forms such as gasoline. Fossil-fuel deposits are limited. As the population grows, demand for energy increase. Fossil fuels are not found everywhere, so they must be shipped to different areas via ships, trucks, and pipelines. Shipping oil can result in oil leaks or spills that pollute the environment.

Facing the Challenge

Today, people all over the world are trying to face the challenges of energy use by focusing on efficiency. By using energy wisely, people can reduce the amount of carbon in the air. By using renewable energy sources, we can reduce our dependence on fossil fuels. By reducing our dependence on fossil fuels, animals and plants can live in a cleaner and healthier environment.

The extraction and refining of fossil fuels is an expensive and energy-consuming process. The process can disrupt natural habitats and hurt animal and plant life.

What Are Fossil Fuels?

Fossil fuels include oil, coal, and natural gas. They are called fossil fuels because they are made of ancient carbon. All living things are made of carbon. The carbon in ancient plants and animals has been compressed underground for millions of years to create coal and oil. When fossil fuels are burned, they release ancient carbon dioxide into the atmosphere.

Global-Warming Debate

Since the 1970s, scientists have reported that Earth's temperature appears to be slowly rising. Scientists believe that humans contributed to the rise in temperature by burning fossil fuels. Many politicians and **economists** were not convinced. Fossil fuels were important to many economies and businesses. It took a long time for people to understand that a change was necessary. During the late 1990s and early 2000s, people began witnessing many of the effects of global warming. Extreme weather, such as flash floods and cold snaps, is the result of shifts in local weather patterns due to changing temperatures. Shifting weather patterns also cause drought, flooding, and intense storms, such as Hurricane Katrina in 2005.

During the 1990s, there were four times as many weather-related disasters as there were during the 1950s. High temperatures melt glaciers, adding more water to the oceans and raising sea levels. Rising sea levels threaten coastal communities, threatening people's homes and livelihoods. Many animal species on land and in the ocean will have to adapt to warmer temperatures and changed habitats or become extinct. As animals look for new habitats, they may also threaten local species, affect communities as pests, and spread diseases.

The flooding caused by Hurricane Katrina in New Orleans, Louisiana, in 2005, was devastating. It left much of the city under water and hundreds of thousands of people homeless.

Changing weather conditions are
causing more and more hurricanes
all over the world. These hurricanes
are extremely destructive and lead
to the loss of life and property.

Carbon Footprint

Every activity has an impact on the environment. Your carbon footprint is a measurement of your impact on Earth and its environments. There are several greenhouse gases, including water vapor, methane, and nitrous oxide. Carbon dioxide is the gas that people have the most control over. A carbon footprint measures your emission of greenhouse gases in units of carbon dioxide. Most people in **developed countries** emit 9 to 11 tons (8 to 10 tonnes) of carbon dioxide every year!

Primary and Secondary

There are two parts to your carbon footprint. Your primary carbon footprint measures the amount of carbon dioxide that is emitted as a result of your personal activities. Driving, heating your home, and using electricity are part of your primary carbon footprint. Your secondary carbon footprint measures the carbon emitted by others who make goods for or provide services to you. The clothes you wear, the food you eat, and the goods you buy, such as video games and electronics, are part of your secondary carbon footprint.

An average male African elephant weighs 12,000 pounds (5,443 kg), or 6 tons (5.4 tonnes). The average North American's annual carbon dioxide output is equivalent to more than two full-grown African elephants.

12

Making a Difference

Why do we measure carbon footprints? Carbon-footprint measurements give us a chance to determine the ways in which we can change our impact on the environment. Global warming is a worldwide issue, and it can be hard to imagine that one person can make a difference to such a big problem. If everyone makes changes, the impact on the environment is significant. With the concrete numbers and details provided by a carbon footprint, we can take action.

Learn about ways in which your transportation affects carbon-dioxide emissions. Can you travel differently to cut back on emissions?

Carbon Footprint Calculator

There are many carbon calculators available online. Visit this website http://www.zerofootprintkids.com/kids_home.aspx to do a basic calculation on your own. Then speak to your parents about completing a more detailed carbon calculation, such as the one at http://www.carbonfootprint.com. You will need a lot of information about electricity bills, gas bills, driving, and energy sources, so it is best to work with a parent. Once you have determined your score, sit down with your family to talk it over. Start setting goals for the future as a team by using the ideas in this book.

Carbon Neutral

When you think about trying to reduce your carbon footprint, your goal should be to become **carbon neutral**. Something that is neutral does not contribute to or take away from. Being carbon neutral means absorbing as much CO_2 as you emit. Carbon neutrality is a balance that you can work toward in two ways. First, you can reduce the amount of carbon dioxide that you emit. Second, you can find ways to absorb CO_2. Tree planting is a great example of finding a way to absorb carbon dioxide. A tree is a carbon sink. Trees absorb and store carbon dioxide. New trees absorb large amounts of carbon dioxide as they grow, which makes tree planting a very effective way of reducing your carbon footprint!

(above) Communities everywhere are starting to shift to a carbon-neutral lifestyle. Planting trees absorbs carbon dioxide, and everyone can help!

CASE STUDY

Carbon Neutral Schools

In 2007, England's government announced that all new high schools would be built with a goal of being carbon neutral. Some schools in the UK had already started working toward a carbon-neutral goal. The Academy of St. Francis Assisi in Liverpool, England, was built to be a carbon-neutral school. The building uses solar power, has desks made of recycled yogurt containers, and has planted gardens that the students look after. In the computer lab, there is a running total of how much energy is being used at any given time, and how much carbon dioxide has not been emitted as a result of the school's policies. The school is not yet carbon neutral, because it is made of concrete. Believe it or not, one ton of carbon dioxide is emitted for every ton of concrete that is produced. However, concrete absorbs and retains heat better than any other building material, which means that the school does not need to depend on heat generated by fossil fuels. The energy savings in heating will eventually balance out the carbon dioxide that was emitted to make the concrete.

But I'm Just a Kid!

Global problems can be tough to think about. It is easy to throw up your hands and give up hope! We all have a role to play, and it is important for each and every person to do his or her part. There are all kinds of things you can do on your own and with your friends and family to make a difference. Everyone makes decisions about how to use energy, which means that your actions can do a great deal to reduce your carbon footprint. So get busy! Join in now to reduce carbon-dioxide emissions and become a carbon-neutral kid.

(above) Use your voice! You may not be old enough to vote, but you can still talk to local politicians at community events. Let them know about your concerns for your community, city, and country.

Conserving Energy

What does electricity have to do with fossil fuels and carbon footprints? Power plants burn coal to generate most electricity. The burning coal heats water, which turns to steam. The steam moves turbines that generate electricity. When you conserve electricity, you reduce the amount of coal that needs to be burned. Find out how your home's electricity is produced. Is any of the energy in your community generated using renewable sources? Does your energy provider, or your gas and electric company, sell energy from a renewable source? It may cost more to buy energy from a renewable source, but it is worth it to save the environment.

Why Conserve Electricity?

Electricity is measured in **watts** and **kilowatts**. The higher the **wattage** of an appliance, the more electricity it needs to run. **High-efficiency** appliances run at the lowest possible wattage. Inefficient appliances waste electricity, causing greenhouse gases to be dumped into the atmosphere. The key to saving electricity is using fewer appliances. Turn off all electrical equipment, including the lights, every time you leave a room. When a light bulb burns out, replace it with a **compact fluorescent bulb**. Remember to read labels and follow instructions for safe disposal of compact fluorescent bulbs.

Compact fluorescent light bulbs use about 75 percent less electricity than regular incandescent bulbs do, and they last about 10 times longer, making them more efficient.

Draining Power

Did you know that your TV, stereo, computer, and game system all use electricity even when they are turned off? Appliances such as these are on standby when they are not in use. They draw power constantly so they are ready whenever you turn them on. Instead of plugging small appliances and electronics into the wall, plug them into an accessible power bar. When not in use, turn off the power bar and unplug it. You have to pull only one plug, but you prevent the power draw of three or four machines. Remember to follow the instructions and safety rules supplied with your power bar. These small steps can help save a lot of electricity and contribute significantly toward reducing pollution levels in the air and the harmful effects of global warming and the greenhouse effect.

Battery Power

Many gadgets today have rechargeable batteries, or batteries that are plugged into the wall to replenish, or reload, power. Rechargeable batteries can be used over and over instead of being tossed into the garbage. They help reduce waste. Be smart about charging batteries, however. Make sure you unplug battery chargers, laptop computers, and cell phones as soon as they have finished charging, so they are not drawing extra power that they cannot store. Remember that all batteries are made up of many dangerous materials, so be sure to dispose of them safely. Many school groups and local governments collect and recycle both rechargeable and non-rechargeable batteries. Solar-powered calculators and wind-up radios do not require batteries, so keep an eye out for these alternatives when shopping for electronics.

Conservation Tip

Solar-powered lights store the sun's energy during the day and light up at night. Use the Internet to find out about solar-powered technologies that might be useful to you and your family.

Big Energy Savings

One of the easiest things any family can do to conserve energy and reduce their carbon footprint is to improve the heating and cooling of their home. Whether your furnace runs on electricity, natural gas, oil, or heated water, you can conserve a great deal of energy by running your furnace efficiently. Here are a few tips: set your thermostat no higher than 68 °F (20 °C) in winter and no lower than 77 °F (25 °C) in summer to keep heating and air conditioning to a minimum. Use air conditioning only when necessary. Keep it turned off at all other times.

Use windows to let the sun warm a house in winter. Keep rooms shaded from the sunlight in summer.

Energy Drain!

Many of the biggest energy drains in a home are large appliances. Refrigerators, ovens, and clothes dryers all use a lot of electricity, especially if they are more than a few years old. While appliances are still in good working order, try these tips to avoid wasting energy. Whenever possible, use the most efficient appliance you have for cooking. Use a toaster oven for small meals or quick reheating. Keep a lid on pots cooking on the stove to keep in heat. Instead of boiling a full kettle, boil only as much water as you need, always being sure to fill the kettle to the minimum amount.

Conservation Tip

Check the seals on all your windows and doors. Drafty windows and doors can let heat escape (or creep in), causing your furnace and air conditioner to run longer than necessary. Replacing windows and doors with energy-efficient versions can also make a big difference!

Refrigerator Rescue

Has a parent ever asked if you were trying to refrigerate the whole neighborhood by leaving the fridge door open? It is a good question! Always close the door, even if you plan to take only a few moments to pour a drink. Let warm food cool down before you put the leftovers into the refrigerator. The cooler food is when it goes in, the easier it is for the fridge to cool it and keep it cold. Just remember not to leave meat, poultry, or eggs at room temperature for more than one hour, since bacteria grow quickly in these foods and they could become unsafe to eat. The coils at the back of the refrigerator release heat inside that is drawn out of the food. When the coils get dusty, the refrigerator has to work harder and longer to release the heat. Vacuum the coils twice a year to keep the refrigerator clean and running at maximum efficiency throughout the year.

Support for Savings

Many local governments encourage people to conserve energy by reducing costs on energy-saving technology. Visit government websites to find out about money-back offers on compact fluorescent light bulbs, or free programs for recycling old refrigerators.

An average clothes dryer uses 500 kilowatts of electricity, so use it as infrequently as possible. Dry clothes outdoors or on drying racks instead of running the dryer.

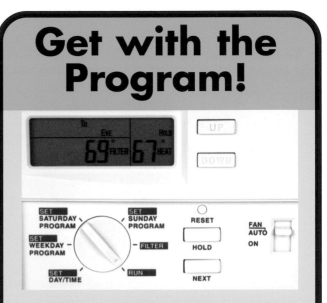

Get with the Program!

A programmable thermostat can also help you cut energy use and costs. Programmable thermostats allow you to set times and temperatures for the furnace or air conditioner. When no one will be in the house, set the temperature a few degrees higher (when cooling) or lower (when heating) than normal. Set a time half an hour before people will return home so the thermostat automatically readjusts the temperature. You can also change the temperature at night, when everyone is sleeping.

Watch Your Hot Water!

It takes a lot of energy to heat water. In fact, heating water is one of the most energy-consuming and expensive tasks we do. One of the problems with heating water is that heat naturally moves toward anything cold, including the ground and the air. For example, the heat in a tub full of hot water escapes quickly into the air above, which may lead bathers to add more hot water. More hot water means more energy. You can reduce your carbon footprint by using less hot water and heating water more efficiently.

Take a shower!

Take short showers instead of long baths. You may use between 16 and 24 gallons (60 and 90 liters) of water for a bath, but a quick shower uses only about 10.5 gallons (40 liters). Baths often require up to 50 percent more hot water than do showers. Talk to your family about installing a low-flow showerhead or a **flow restrictor** to conserve hot water. This device on your showerhead reduces the flow of water.

Clothes washing

Wash clothes in cold water instead of warm water. Some types of dirt, such as oily stains, may require a hot water wash. Most clothes, however, will be just as clean in a cold water wash. Front-loading washing machines use much less water. They are also much more energy efficient. Be sure to look for an EnergyStar labeled machine.

Logos such as the Energy Star help shoppers identify energy-efficient appliances.

Showerhead timers keep showers on a tight schedule by controlling the hot water used.

If you do not have an automatic dishwasher, try to reduce hot water use by rinsing soapy dishes in a bowl of warm water instead of running them under the faucet. Pouring water from a bowl to rinse several dishes at once can also reduce hot-water waste. Ask your parents to invest in an insulating blanket for your hot-water heater. Most hot-water heaters are in cool basements, and they lose heat into the air around them, wasting energy. By insulating the tank with a specially designed blanket, you use less energy.

(right) Insulation covering a water heater reduces the amount of energy needed to heat the water.

(below) Remind family members to turn off the faucet when brushing their teeth or shaving.

Planes, Trains, and Cars

In North America, we burn a lot of fossil fuel traveling from one place to another. Cars, buses, trucks, and airplanes all dump greenhouse gases into the atmosphere. If you can cut down the time you spend in vehicles, you can help reduce your carbon footprint. In other words, using your real footprints can make a big difference to your carbon footprint!

Two Feet and a Heartbeat

Can you walk or bike to school, to a friend's house, or to the corner store? Can you organize a group of friends to walk to school together with a parent or supervisor? If you are not able to organize a walking or biking pool, a carpool will also cut down on energy. If three families send their children to school in one car instead of three, two fewer cars are on the road. School buses are a type of carpool, so they can help reduce emissions, too.

Buses, Trains, and Subways

Public transportation is a good way to cut back on fossil fuel use. Many people in bigger cities use public transit, such as buses, trains, and subways, to get to and from school and work. By not driving themselves, they keep many cars off the road. Cities all over the world are also exploring alternative fuels for city buses. **Biodiesel** is fuel made from natural substances such as plants. **Hydrogen fuel cells** use a chemical reaction between hydrogen and oxygen to generate power. Most city buses run on fossil fuels, but if they ran on biofuel or another renewable resource, emissions would be cut even lower. Let your parents, teachers, and local politicians know that you would like your city to invest in cleaner public transit for the good of everyone in your community.

Air travel is a big issue when it comes to carbon footprints.
Planes use a lot of fossil fuels and emit carbon monoxide.

Buy Local Products

When your family buys groceries, do you shop at a local market or at a big food store? Big supermarket chains often import food, such as fresh fruit, from all over the world. Importing means a lot of fossil fuel use. Trains, planes, and trucks carry food from warm climates to cool climates. They emit a lot of carbon dioxide. Try to buy local produce, eggs, dairy, and meat products whenever possible. These items have not been driven many miles to reach you, which reduces carbon-dioxide emissions.

(above) Support the environment and local farmers by buying produce at a local market.

CASE STUDY

Meatless meals

Do you have a promising chef in your family? Ask him or her to find recipes for healthy, balanced meals without meat. Try to eat a meal with no meat two or three times a week. Many forests are cleared to raise cattle for large, international food producers. By cutting down on the meat you eat, you can help reduce the demand for large cattle farms.

Consume Less

You and your family are consumers. You buy goods and use them. Can consuming less reduce your carbon footprint? You are probably familiar with the three Rs: reduce, reuse, and recycle. These three practices can work together to reduce your **consumption**, or the amount you consume, which, in turn, reduces your carbon footprint. Reducing means consuming less. Reusing means wasting less. Recycling means breaking down something so it can be used again.

Reduce

Plastics are petroleum-based products, which means they are made from oil. If you take a look around your home, you will see plastic everywhere, from your computer monitor to your iron to your food containers. Plastics do not cost very much money, which means that they are often used instead of natural materials. By using less plastic, you can reduce your carbon footprint. Volunteer to help with family grocery shopping. Look for products with the least amount of packaging. Talk to your parents about shopping at bulk-food stores. Ask them to bring reusable glass or ceramic containers to the store. The store clerk will measure the containers when they are empty, and then subtract the weight of the container to determine how much of each product you are purchasing.

Bottle Fed

Reducing or giving up bottled water is an easy way to reduce your carbon footprint, because it requires fossil fuels to make the plastic bottles and ship them around the world. Most tap water is as clean as or cleaner than bottled water, because it is treated in local water treatment plants. Use refillable water containers instead of plastic bottles. Bottled water is only good for one year after it is bottled, because chemicals in the plastic may start to leach into the water after a length of time. Using tap water is easier, less expensive, and better for the planet!

Reuse

Think creatively about ways in which you could reduce consumption by reusing items. Always remember to clean things properly before reusing them, especially if you are storing food. Rinse out empty yogurt and margarine containers and their lids to use for storage. If you do not yet have cloth bags for groceries, bring used plastic bags to the store or market and reuse them whenever possible. Get creative when wrapping gifts by using old magazines, newspapers, and odds and ends of cloth and ribbon.

If your family has a computer printer, ask everyone to save one-sided printouts that they no longer need. As long as the information is not private, the paper can be reused on the other side. You can make your own scratchpads by cutting the paper into interesting shapes and stapling the sheets together.

Some grocery stores sell reusable cloth bags for carrying groceries. The bags are also good for carrying books!

Conservation Tip

Stop using plastic for shopping. Use cloth bags instead. You can make your own cloth bag by taking scraps of cloth lying about in your house and stitching them together.

25

(above) The recycling symbol is three arrows wrapping a triangle or Earth.

(below) Recycling is the third R because it should be your third choice. After you have reduced your consumption and reused items as much as possible, it is time to recycle them.

Recycle

Most cities and towns collect recyclable materials along with trash. It is usually up to each family to sort the recyclable materials and put them in a separate container for the collectors. Some items are not recyclable, and local recycling programs do not accept some other items. One non-recyclable item can ruin a whole batch of recycling, so it is important to be aware. Learn all the details of your local program. If you have any questions, call the recycling depot and ask. Then volunteer to set up a recycling center in the garage, the basement, or a kitchen cupboard. Put yourself in charge of sorting paper, plastic, glass, and metal recyclables.

Paper is made from trees, which store carbon dioxide. When trees are processed into paper, the carbon dioxide stored in the trees is released into the environment. Reduce your paper use, reuse as much paper as you can, and recycle what is left.

Making the Change

People all over the world are learning more about their carbon footprints and the role of fossil fuels in everyday life. As their awareness increases, emissions will be reduced. What can your school, town, region, and country do?

Local Solutions

Schools, neighborhoods, villages, and cities around the world are stating their goals to go carbon neutral. People living in condominiums work together to reduce emissions from their buildings. American universities such as South New Hampshire University and Middlebury College in Vermont have also pledged to become carbon neutral by reducing consumption and using alternative energy sources.

Even large corporations, such as Yahoo!, have pledged to become carbon neutral. In 2007, China announced plans to create Dongtan Eco-City, a carbon-neutral island. The island will have a habitat for migrating birds, solar power, rain collecting and purifying, and clean fuels for vehicles.

Ideas for the Future

Scientists and economists have suggested several ways in which local, national, and international governments can help reduce carbon emissions. One is to reduce or remove **subsidies** on fossil fuels. Subsidies are amounts of money that are given to suppliers of fossil fuels to keep prices to the consumers low. Low prices make people reluctant to stop using fossil fuels. If people knew how much fossil fuels actually cost, they might find it easier to acknowledge the environmental cost as well. Another suggestion is to put a tax on carbon emissions to force individuals, businesses, corporations, and governments to pay for the carbon they emit. Everyone would then try to emit less to save money. Governments can also stop people from cutting down forests, and protect carbon sinks such as forests, bogs, and oceans.

Around the world, businesses and corporations are using alternative energy sources more frequently. Every step counts! Solar panels on buildings store the sun's energy. The energy is converted into power, which is used by many companies.

Climate Conferences

Governments around the world started working together in 1997 in Kyoto, Japan, to address the problem of carbon-dioxide emissions and the effects of global warming. It was difficult to agree on a course of action. Some countries believed that reductions were the responsibility mostly of developed countries. Others believed that everyone had to play a role to prevent natural disasters, overcrowding, and famine, or food shortages, due to climate change. Many countries committed to the Kyoto Protocol, the treaty that was developed during these meetings. A few large countries, including the United States, refused to commit or to follow through on their commitment to the treaty.

In late 2007, 187 nations attended the U.N. Climate Conference in Bali, Indonesia. At this conference, countries negotiated ways to meet their targets for reducing emissions. Important talks focused on limiting cutting down forests and regrowing forests where possible, especially in developing countries. At the end of the conference, the delegates agreed to negotiate a new treaty by the end of 2009. This treaty will replace the Kyoto Protocol, which expires at the end of 2012. The new treaty will focus on immediate action, support for the least-developed countries as they cut emissions, and targets that can be enforced by international law.

At the 2007 United Nations Conference on Climate Change in Bali, a new treaty was made to cut carbon emissions.

Timeline

Scientists have speculated since the late 1800s that carbon-dioxide emissions increase Earth's temperature. Not until the 1900s did they realize that humans and human consumption habits contribute to global warming, or the gradual warming of Earth's atmosphere.

Many American cities have begun utilizing hybrid technology for public transportation.

Organizations like Oxfam (above) stage protests in the hopes of saving the environment.

1824

French mathematician Joseph Fourier calculates that Earth's temperature is slowly rising.

1896

Swedish scientist Svente Arrhenius develops a theory that carbon dioxide emissions, increased by burning fossil fuels, might alter the temperature by trapping solar heat near Earth's surface.

1930s

Rising temperatures make people begin to wonder if the planet is getting warmer. The shift is dismissed as part of a natural cycle.

1954

Biologist G. Evelyn Hutchison suggests that clearing forests will also affect the levels of carbon dioxide.

1960s

Climate researchers find new ways of learning about the climate in ancient times. This research is used to determine patterns in the climate.

1961

Science shows that carbon dioxide can build up in the atmosphere, possibly with warming effects. Tests show that the level of carbon dioxide in the atmosphere is increasing.

1970s

The environmental movement encourages people to think about the effects of their activities on the natural world.

1979

First World Climate Conference discusses climate change.

1988

The hottest summer on record until that time. The Intergovernmental Panel on Climate Change (IPCC) is formed.

1992

The United Nations Framework Convention on Climate Change is created at the Rio Earth Summit.

1997

Kyoto Protocol adopted in Japan on December 11.

2001

The IPCC publicizes a statement that it is likely that climate change is occurring and should be addressed.

2001-2005

Countries agree to uphold the Kyoto Protocol; the United States, the nation with the largest emissions, refuses.

2003

Europe experiences its hottest summer in 500 years.

2005

Australian author Tim Flannery publishes *The Weather Makers: How We Are Changing the Climate and What it Means for Life on Earth*, a best-selling book about the science and urgency of global warming.

2006

Former U.S. Vice President Al Gore stars in *An Inconvenient Truth*, a documentary film of his presentations on global warming.

2007

The IPCC releases its Fourth Assessment Report stating that temperatures could rise by nearly 11°F (6°C) by the end of the century if direct action is not taken; IPCC and Al Gore awarded Nobel Peace Prize; UN Climate Conference held in Bali puts together a treaty to replace the Kyoto Protocol when it ends.

Al Gore, former US Vice-President, received a Nobel Prize for his work on global warming, which includes the documentary film, AnInconvenient Truth.

Glossary

carbon sinks   Forests, oceans, or bogs that store carbon that is not being used in nature

compact fluorescent bulb   A light bulb designed to use less power, last longer, and give the same light as a candescent light bulb

developed countries   Countries with modern economies and good standards of living such as the United States and Canada

economists   People who study the careful use of resources such as money

famine   Shortage of food

flow restrictor   A device that can limit the amount of water that flows from a showerhead or faucet

fossil fuels   Fuels found in Earth's crust that are non-renewable sources of energy

global warming   An increase in the temperature of Earth's atmosphere, especially for a sustained amount of time

greenhouse gas   Gases in the atmosphere that absorb heat from Earth's surface

high-efficiency   Describes something (a machine) that uses the lowest possible wattage of electricity

hydrogen fuel cells   Electrochemical devices that combine hydrogen and oxygen to produce power such as electricity

kilowatts   A unit of power equal to 1,000 watts

kinetic energy   Energy that is formed as a result of motion

natural gas   A gaseous fossil fuel that is used to produce fuel for power

non-renewable   Resources with a limited supply, such as fossil fuels

radioactive waste   Waste containing radioactive material; it is often the result of generating nuclear energy

renewable   Resources with an unlimited supply, such as wind, sun, and water

subsidies   Amounts of money given to oil suppliers to help keep costs of oil low for consumers

wattage   The amount of power a machine needs in order to run

watts   Units used to measure electricity

Index